Elevator

A box that transports people or objects to different floors of a building (1852 -1854)

Typewriter

A device like a keyboard that prints letters when you press buttons, which is neater than handwriting (1868)

Lightbulb

A device which uses electricity to create light without using a flame (1879)

Automobile

The first horseless carriage that travelled using a gasoline engine (1886)

The Young Inventor

Born in Scotland in 1847, Alexander Graham Bell grew up fascinated with inventing. At only age 12, he invented his first useful device: a contraption made from nail brushes and paddles that could remove the husks from wheat more quickly and efficiently, to help his neighbor who ran a flour mill.

The Science of Speech

Alexander became very interested in acoustics when his mother gradually lost her hearing and wanted to find ways to continue to communicate with her through tapping his fingers and using the vibrations of his voice. His father, an elocutionist, was thrilled by Alexander's interest and encouraged his studies of the science of sound. He even funded Alexander and his two brothers' personal project to make a talking automaton (robot) head. The science of speech became Alexander's focus in life, and he dedicated many years to working with deaf and mute individuals, offering speech therapy and teaching sign language and lip reading.

The Great Telephone

While he worked, Alexander liked to experiment with inventing new things. He created a phonautograph, a machine that could draw the shape of sound waves on a sheet of smoke-coated glass by tracing their vibrations—using the bones from the ear of a dead man. This invention made him wonder if he could create electrical currents that corresponded to sound waves, and over years of research and development, he used this idea to invent the first working telephone.

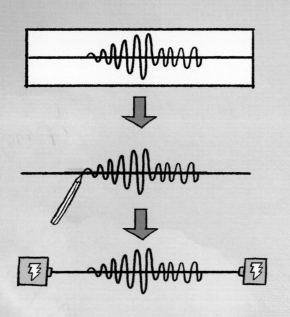

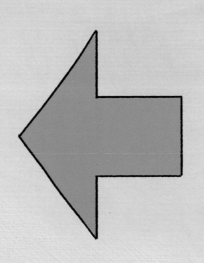

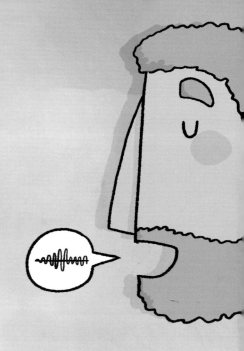

Contributing to a number of important inventions such as the metal detector and the airplane, Alexander played a big part in the rise of technology in the 19th century. His most well-known invention was, of course, the telephone, but what Alexander didn't know was that he wasn't the only one inventing it at the time.

We're not here to talk about Alexander today. We're here to talk about the SECOND person in the world to invent the telephone . . . and that was a man named Elisha Gray.

This book is dedicated to my Nan. Also Aofie, Anna, Amy, Katie, Laura, and Megan. You guys rock.

It is not dedicated to Steve. I don't know a Steve, this book is not dedicated to you.

This Book Belongs To

_ _ _ _ _ _ _ _ _ _ _ _ _

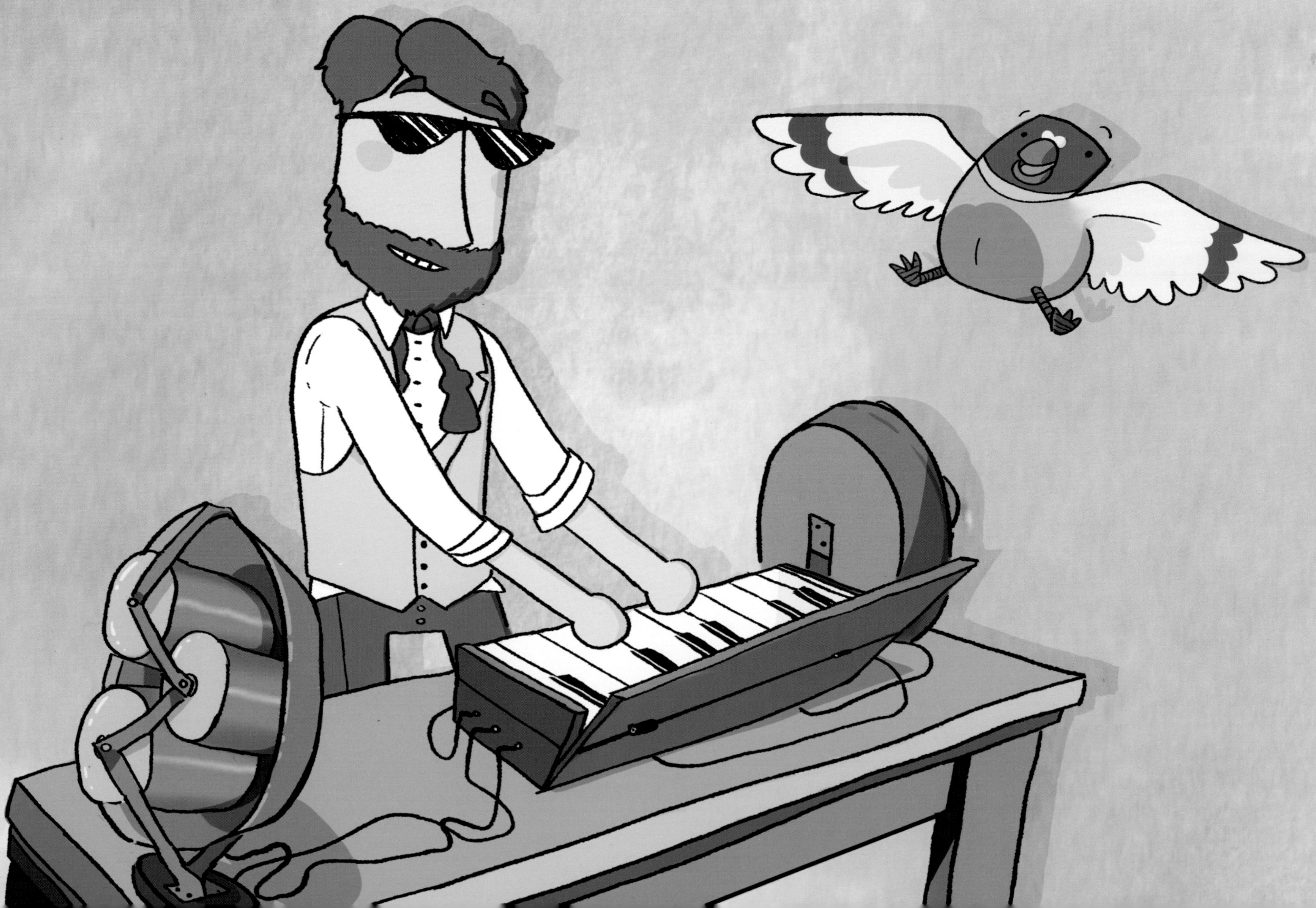

Published by Yeehoo Press
6540 Lusk Blvd, Ste C152, San Diego, CA 92121
www.yeehoopress.com

Edited by Jiahui Zhu
Designed by Si Ye
Original concept by Zhiqiao Wang
Supervised by Luyang Xue
Library of Congress Control Number: 2022931560
ISBN: 978-1-953458-40-7
Printed in China First Edition
1 2 3 4 5 6 7 8 9 10

THE SECOND IN THE WORLD

to Invent the Telephone: *Elisha Gray*

By Farren Phillips

YEEHOO PRESS

Contents

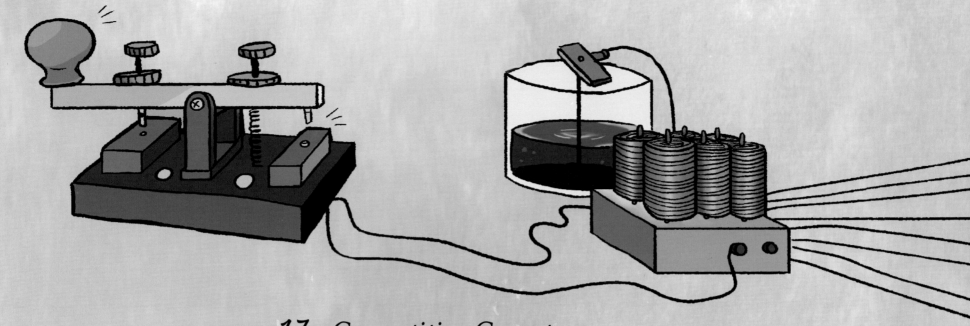

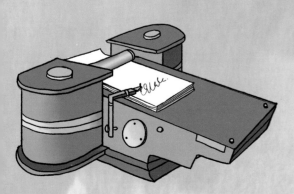

EARLY LIFE FOR ELISHA

As a boy, Elisha lived with his mother and father on a farm in Ohio. Elisha loved school and was interested in science, but at only 12 years old, he had to leave school and go to work on the farm to help support himself and his mother after his father passed away.

ELISHA'S ESCAPADES

Elisha took on work as an apprentice blacksmith, a carpenter, and a dairy farmer. He was never very successful at manual labor, and as hard as poor Elisha worked, he barely seemed to make enough money to live on.

At age 22, Elisha went back to school to try to get a formal education. He still had to work while studying, even becoming a janitor at the school and building equipment for the science department. He was so worn out from balancing work and school that he became ill and exhausted and ended up leaving again without graduating.

INITIAL INVENTION

The setback, however, didn't stop Elisha from pursuing his interest in science. Even while working on the dairy farm and after settling down to get married, the school let him continue using their electronic equipment to keep experimenting and learning in his free time.

That's when Elisha patented his very first invention—the self-adjusting telegraph relay!

Back in those days, they didn't have phones or computers yet, so getting messages to people really quickly was very hard. A machine called the telegraph made this easier. It was a device that could transmit electrical signals across a wire stretched between different telegraph stations, sending a message in Morse code from one location to the next in mere minutes.

MORSE MADNESS

What is Morse Code?

Well, with telegraphs, they could only send beeps from one place to another, not letters or words. So how do you communicate with only beeps? Morse code was a language invented to turn beep patterns into letters. A short beep is a dot, and a long beep is a dash. The Morse code alphabet looks like this, so if you wanted to send the word "Hello," you'd actually have to tap the pattern .... . .—.. .—.. ———, and the person on the other end of the line would decode it into letters.

Can you write your name using Morse code?

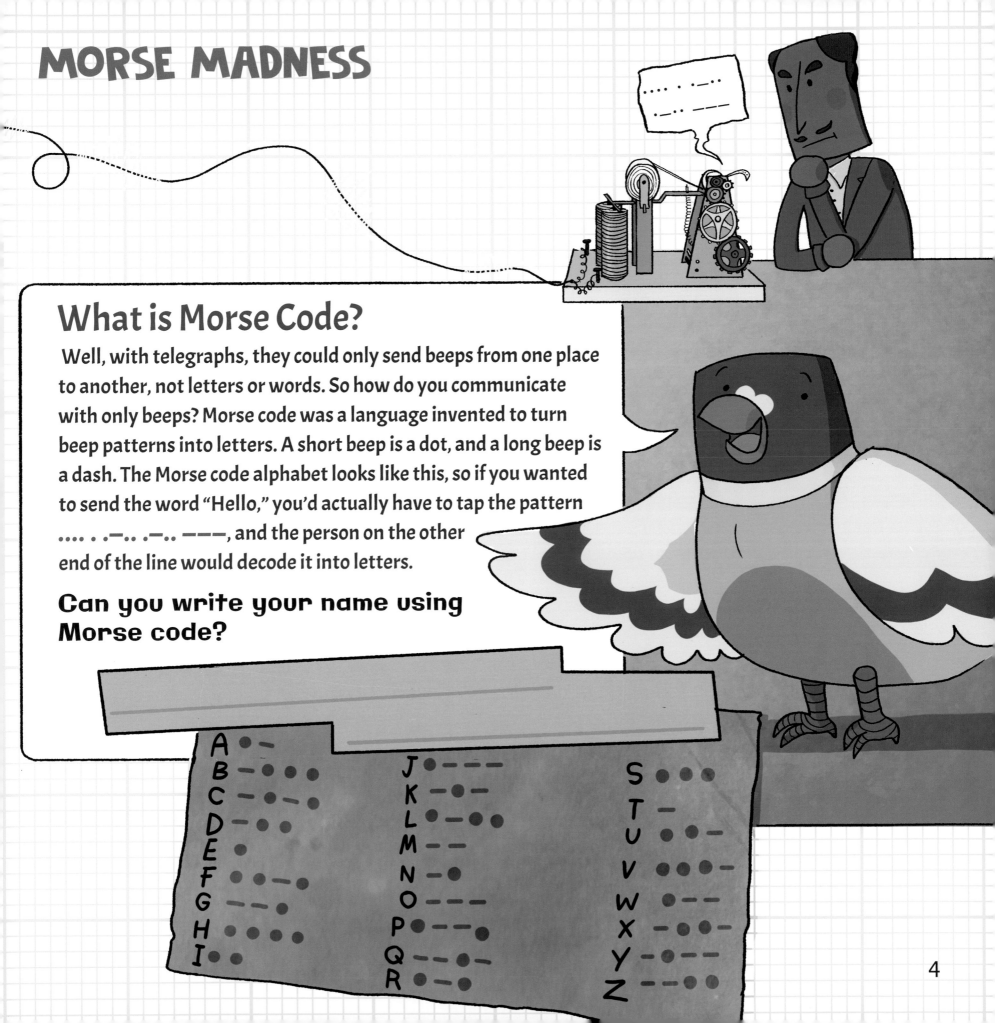

A ·—
B —···
C —·—·
D —··
E ·
F ··—·
G ——·
H ····
I ··

J ·———
K —·—
L ·—··
M ——
N —·
O ———
P ·——·
Q ——·—
R ·—·

S ···
T —
U ··—
V ···—
W ·——
X —··—
Y —·——
Z ——··

WHAT IS A SELF-ADJUSTING TELEGRAPH RELAY?

Electric signals would weaken over time, and the telegraph messages would sometimes get lost over long distance wires. Imagine the electrical signal being like a delivery man who has to run the message from one location to another and sometimes gets too tired to make it to his destination. A relay is a device that resets the message at intervals. It's like our little delivery man can pass the message onto a new delivery man at every stop on the route, meaning he won't overexert himself and the message will arrive safely.

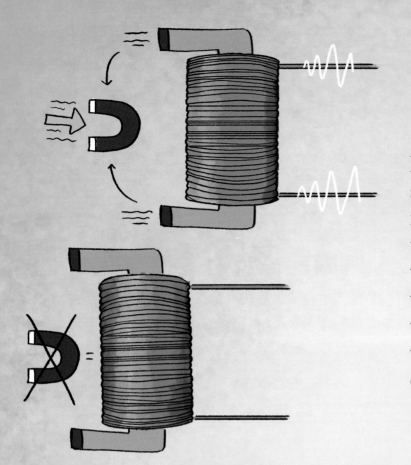

Elisha reinvented the relay device to be automatic, so a person at each interval wouldn't need to resend the message. He figured out that he could use electromagnetic coils to automatically repeat the message for each electrical signal that passed through. An electromagnetic coil is a copper coil that becomes a magnet when electricity passes through it, but stops being a magnet when the electricity stops flowing.

Elisha's automatic relay worked by having an electromagnetic coil open and close a circuit. When the electric pulse for a dot or a dash passed through the coil, it would become a magnet and make the gate on another circuit close through magnetic attraction; when the pulse stopped, there was no more magnetic attraction and the gate on the other circuit would open again. A fresh power source connected to the new circuit would repeat the same Morse code pattern with the taps of the gate opening and closing. Every time the gate closed it would allow a pulse of electricity to go through—a long pulse was a dash and a short pulse was a dot. Imagine a magnet and a spring having a tug of war over a bridge—when the magnet pulls one way, the electricity can cross the bridge, and when the spring pulls the other way, it can't.

ELISHA AND ENOS

Elisha started working with a man called Enos M. Barton, who owned an electrical engineering business in Ohio. They took up business together making telegraph equipment for the Western Union Telegraph Company, the biggest telegraph company in America at the time. Elisha created a new kind of telegraph with a typewriter keyboard attachment that allowed people not versed in Morse code to send and receive telegraph messages.

Elisha and Enos called their company Graybar Electric Company (a mix of their surnames, Gray and Barton), and a few years later, the work they were doing was so successful that Western Union decided to buy a third of the company and renamed it Western Electric Manufacturing Company, which remained in business for over 100 years.

Being the chief engineer for an electrical company paid much better than being a dairy farmer, but it still wasn't quite what Elisha wanted to do with his life.

THE SCIENCE OF SOUND

He wanted to invent more things to help improve the telegraph industry and had some ideas for a telegraph machine that could transmit sound instead of code.

But what is sound exactly?

The sounds you hear are made by vibrations transmitted by invisible waves. Although we can't see them with the naked eye, they look different depending on the type of sound. For example:

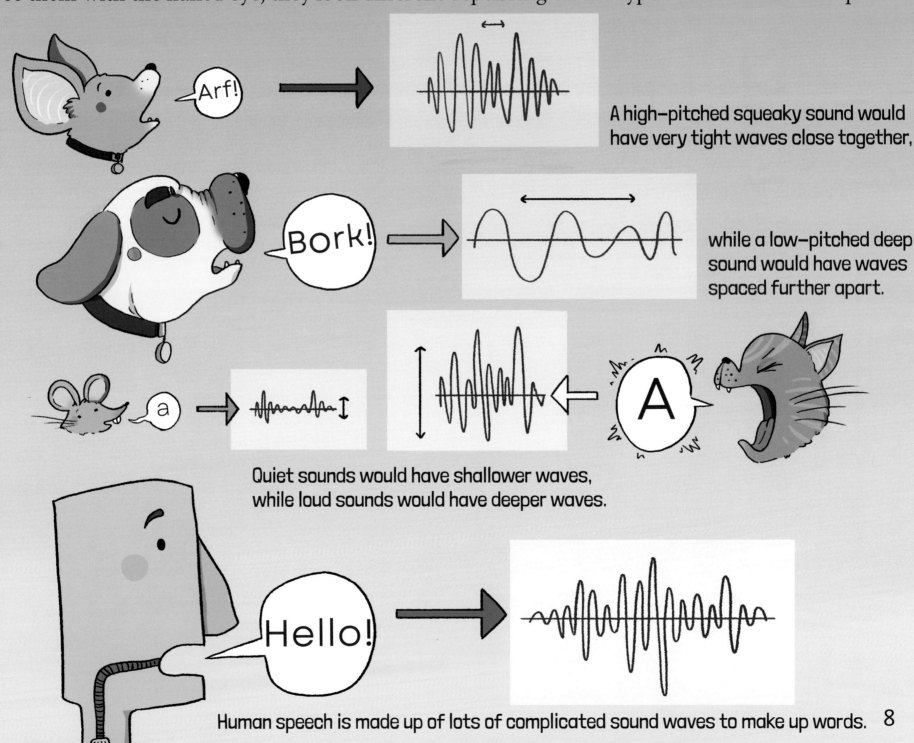

A high-pitched squeaky sound would have very tight waves close together,

while a low-pitched deep sound would have waves spaced further apart.

Quiet sounds would have shallower waves, while loud sounds would have deeper waves.

Human speech is made up of lots of complicated sound waves to make up words.

WONDERING ABOUT WAVES

Elisha knew that speech was a complicated—much more complicated than recreating single-note dots and dashes with electrical waves. Creating a telegraph that could make multiple recognizable notes or even speech was a huge project.

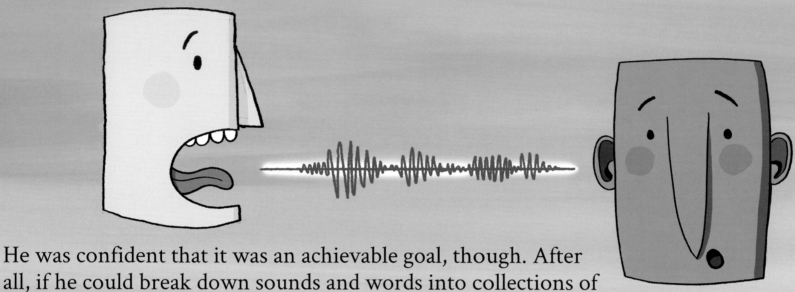

He was confident that it was an achievable goal, though. After all, if he could break down sounds and words into collections of individual waves and recreate them, surely he could piece them back together and get the original sound.

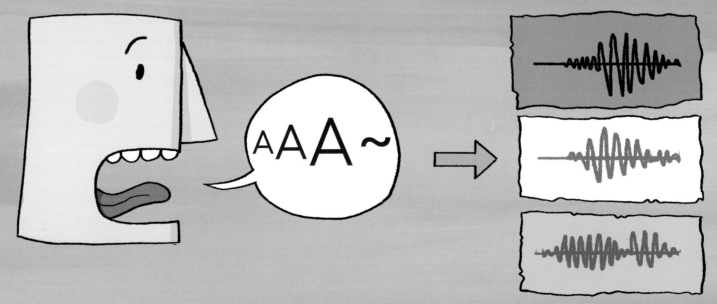

Determined to make his dream a reality, Elisha started dedicating his time to trying to make this ambitious project come to life. Inventing was an expensive business, though, and in order to invent things, Elisha needed a lot more money. He had to get someone to fund his research.

WHAT IS FUNDING?

It was common for rich gentlemen to fund the research of inventors with their masses of money, and it still is today. It's referred to as "investment," and the idea is that you put a small amount of money into helping something to get invented.

The inventor uses the money to make their creation come to life. If the invention is successful, people will buy it, and the inventor will make lots of money.

The inventor then gives the investor a portion of their new riches, and the investor gets even more money than they started out with. It is a gamble, because if the invention were to fail and people didn't buy it, the investor could lose money.

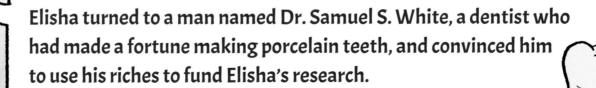

Elisha turned to a man named Dr. Samuel S. White, a dentist who had made a fortune making porcelain teeth, and convinced him to use his riches to fund Elisha's research.

BATHTUBS AND BATTERIES

Transmitting sound through an
electric telegraph was unheard of and a
big task to take on. Elisha first started with
musical instruments rather than voices.

Elisha's breakthrough came to him when his young
nephew was playing around with his equipment. The little
boy had discovered that if he rubbed a battery on the side of his
empty bath tub, it would make a humming sound. Elisha realized
that he could control sound by using a self-vibrating electromagnetic
circuit, which meant that he could create a single note by transmitting
vibrations through electricity.

THE FIRST ELECTRIC PIANO

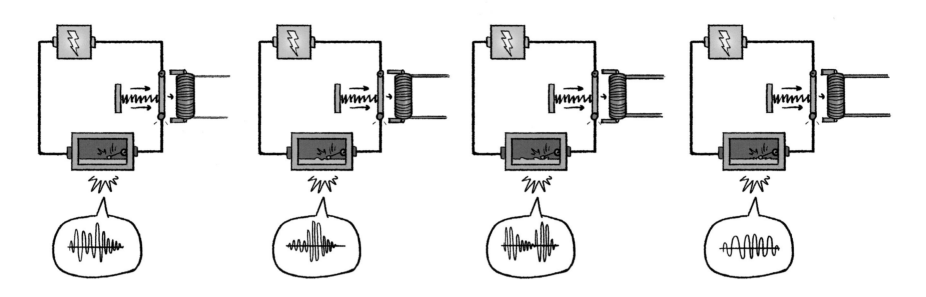

Using a different circuit for different notes, Elisha realized that if he combined multiple circuits together in one relay machine, he could send songs rather than single notes. This was when he invented the musical telegraph keyboard transmitter. It looked like a small piano, but beneath each key was a tuned reed. When the key was pressed and the circuit was complete, an electric current would vibrate the reed and produce a note.

The tunes he played on the musical telegraph could be transmitted through a wire to a regular receiver, or to a special receiver that he invented called the washbasin receiver, which amplified the sound to fill a room—a little like a loudspeaker.

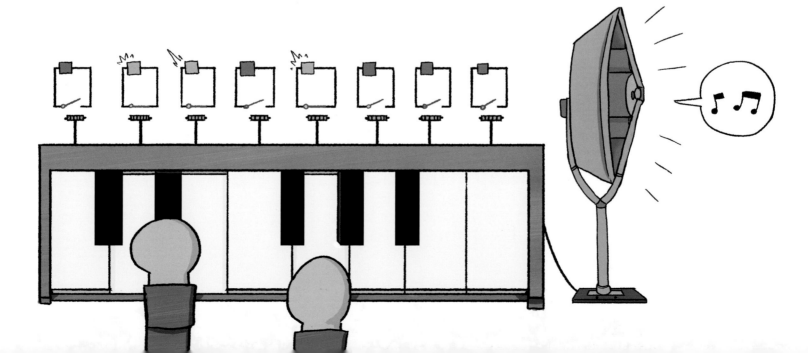

SCIENCE AND SONGS

Excited by his new invention, Elisha put on a public demonstration in 1874 at the Presbyterian Church in Highland Park, Illinois. He wowed the audience by having familiar tunes played through his device for all to hear, all transmitted with electricity!

The show was so successful that later that year, he took his musical telegraph with him on tour all the way to the UK, and showed the public that his device could transmit music through wires over 200 miles apart.

Oh no! It looks like the telegraph wires have gotten very tangled. Can you figure out which receiver is going to play the music?

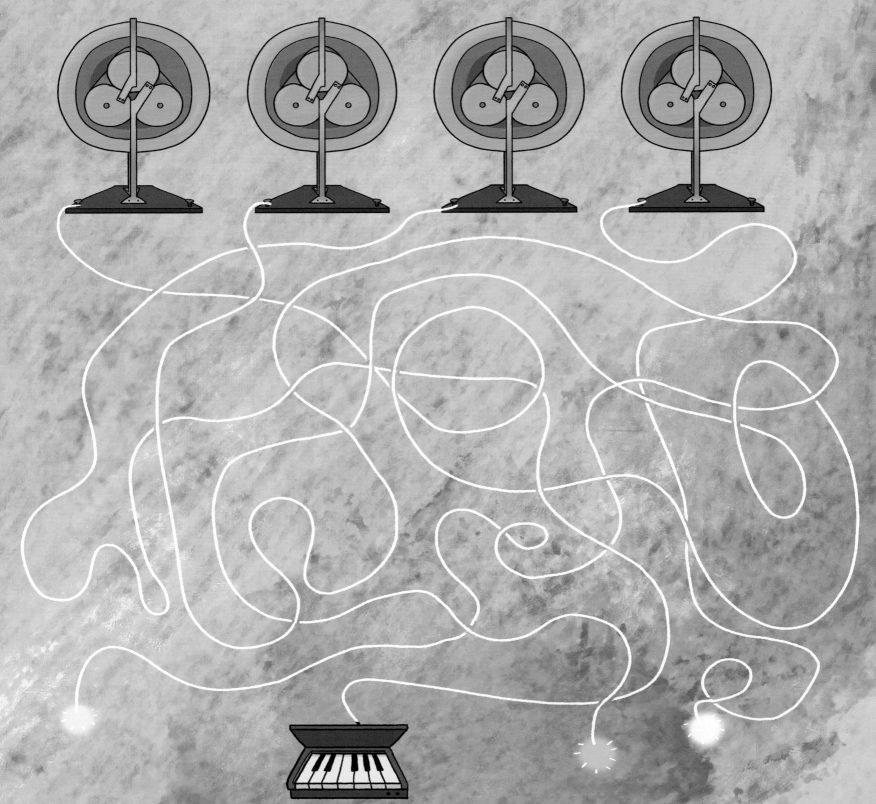

THE BIG BREAKTHROUGH

Motivated by his musical success, Elisha started working on a new device for creating sounds through electricity called a liquid transmitter. It was sort of like a drum: when sound hit the surface, it created vibrations that were picked up by a needle. The vibrations would vary the strength of an electrical current passing through the metal needle from a battery. These differing electrical currents would be transferred through a wire, and then reversed back into vibrations on the other side.

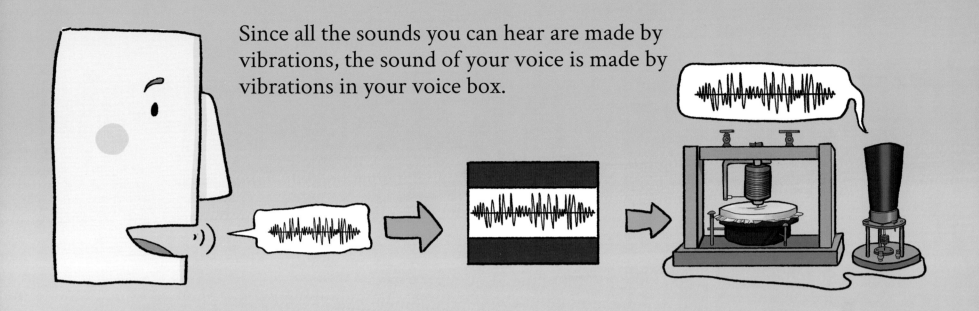

Since all the sounds you can hear are made by vibrations, the sound of your voice is made by vibrations in your voice box.

Elisha figured out that when the vibrations traveling through the air hit a surface, they would make the surface vibrate too. Liquids like water create movements and ripples when hit by vibrations. So he could use a surface touching a liquid to record sound waves.

If he could record the vibrations of a complex sound or voice using a drum-like material stretched over a body of liquid, convert those vibrations into electric pulses, and manage to convert those electronic pulses back into sound waves, he could transport sounds and words from one location to another no matter how far away.

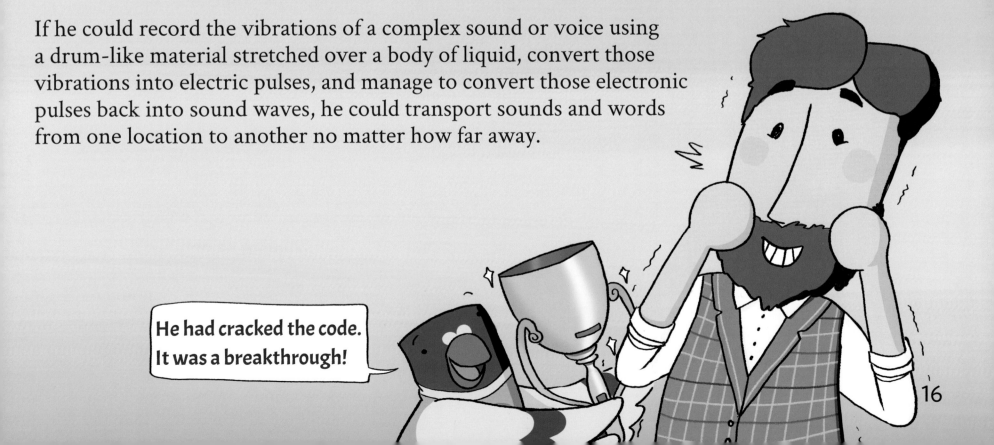

He had cracked the code. It was a breakthrough!

16

COMPETITIVE CAVEAT

Elisha was confident that his new device would finally open up the world of telegraphs to spoken voices, so in February of 1876, he applied for a caveat (which was similar to a patent application but without the examination request) for his newest and greatest invention.

Unfortunately, what Elisha didn't know was that on that very same day, someone else had submitted a patent application for the telephone too. . . .

The examiners have a lot of patent applications to work through.
Can you help them out by counting how many there are on this page?

SCIENTIST SHOW-OFFS

Centennial Exhibition

Later that year, in 1876, a huge event called the Centennial Exhibition was happening in Pennsylvania. It was the very first of many World's Fairs. Inventors from all around could come and show off their amazing inventions and discoveries, and America could show off their industrial prowess to the rest of the world.

THE IMPRESSIVE INVENTOR

Elisha had filed a caveat for his liquid transmitter, but he hadn't had time to build one yet. Instead, he wowed the judges with a multiple telegraphs device. Sending eight telegraph messages at the same time, his invention was a big success! People were amazed—it had never been done before, and they were very impressed by Elisha . . .

THE (MUCH MORE) IMPRESSIVE INVENTOR

. . . Until another inventor, Alexander Graham Bell, revealed his new device—the telephone!

Yes that's right, Alexander took the spotlight of the show when he showed off the very same invention that Elisha had been trying to make.

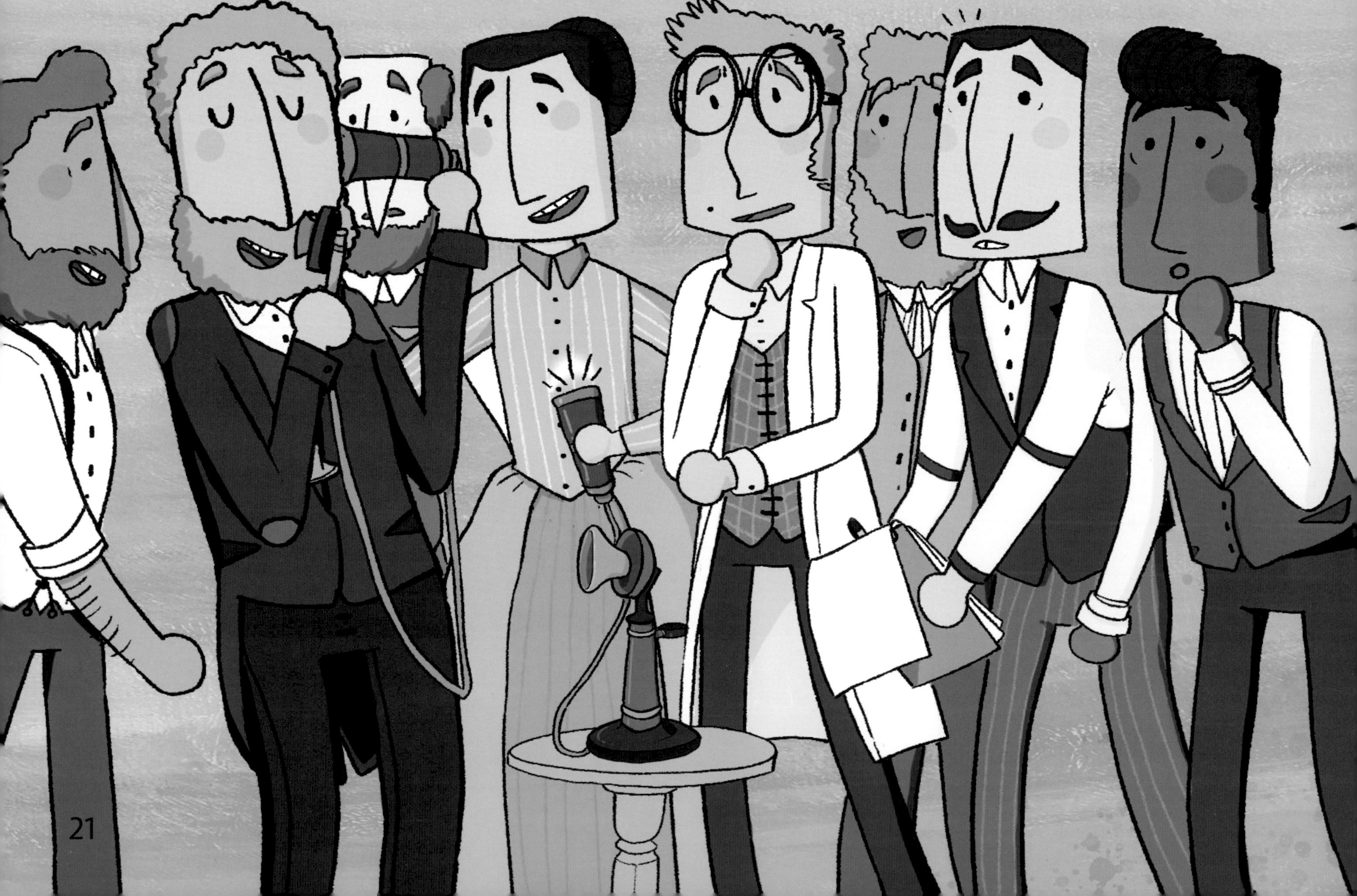

The crowd instantly left Elisha in the dust to flock around Alexander, in awe of his incredible machine that could transmit human voices. Everyone wanted to catch a glimpse of the amazing invention. Even the Emperor of Brazil, a man named Dom Pedro II, was famously so floored by the presentation that he loudly proclaimed:

"My God, it talks!"

DISMAY AND DISPUTES

So what is the truth? Did Alexander steal Elisha's idea, or was their simultaneous discovery a coincidence?

Elisha was upset and felt his idea had been stolen. Thus launched a long legal case between the two, arguing over who had really invented the phone first and if Alexander had stolen Elisha's ideas.

There is still controversy around who deserved credit for the invention of the telephone, and Elisha and Alexander were not even the only two inventors at the time developing similar technology.

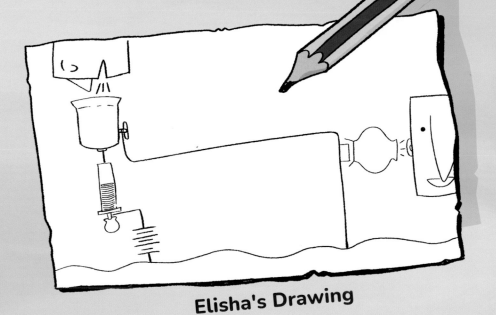

Elisha's Drawing

While Alexander hadn't initially mentioned liquid transmitters in his patent application for the telephone, he had previously drawn up many patents for other inventions that used liquid transmitters. Looking back on Alexander's history of inventions, it's easy to see how his previous inventions led up to the telephone.

However, Elisha had submitted an illustration of his telephone concept on his patent caveat in February of that year, and Alexander was recorded to have sketched a strikingly similar illustration in his own notebook in March, a month later. There was an accusation that Alexander had paid a patent office examiner named Wilber $100 to show him Elisha's caveat paperwork. Alexander swore this was not true, though Wilber was discredited as being a liar when his story didn't quite add up.

Alexander's Drawing

In the end, Alexander was awarded the patent along with the title of inventor of the telephone. His and Elisha's patents had enough differences between them that it was determined that Alexander did not steal Elisha's ideas, and the case was finally dropped.

RIDICULOUS RACE RUSE

A common myth about Elisha and Alexander is that the two of them raced to the patent office only for Alexander to arrive first, and that is why he was awarded the patent and not Elisha.

This didn't happen, although they did both submit their patents on the same day—the 14th of February. In fact, Elisha submitted his caveat a few hours before Alexander submitted his application. The patent was awarded to the first person to invent the device, not the first person to file the application, so it wouldn't have mattered either way.

The race is on! How quickly can you find the route to the patent office?

START

Patent Office

26

THE PERSISTENT PIANIST

Although disgruntled he wouldn't receive credit for his greatest invention and passion project, Elisha never stopped inventing. Reluctantly leaving his telephone ideas in the past, he returned to his musical transmitter once more, developing it further and continuing to show it off to the world.

In 1877, he put on an entire concert in New York City, hiring a famous pianist named Frederick Boscovitz to play beautiful melodies on his new and improved sixteen note musical telegraph—from Philadelphia! It turned out well, with hundreds of people flocking to listen to the electronic melodies, and Elisha even did five more concerts following it.

However, it was widely referred to as a novelty, something fun rather than practical. The device wasn't hailed as a life-changing invention that would revolutionize the world—like the telephone was.

ELISHA'S INVENTIONS

Over the course of his life, Elisha was awarded 70 patents for devices he created. In his final years, he started developing an underwater signaling device that could send messages to ships at sea, but only a year after starting, in 1901, he passed away. The invention was given to Oberlin College where he had studied so that students could continue working on it.

Elisha invented many interesting devices over the course of his career, including but not limited to:

A needle annunciator for elevators, a device that points to a number corresponding to the floor the elevator is currently stopped on

A microphone printer with a typewriter attached that printed messages onto a strip of paper

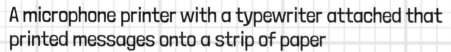

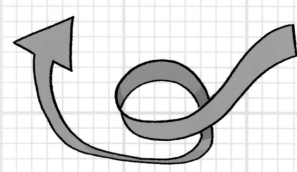

A musical telegraph, the first kind of electric musical instrument that used vibrating electromagnetic circuits and operated via piano keys to transmit different notes

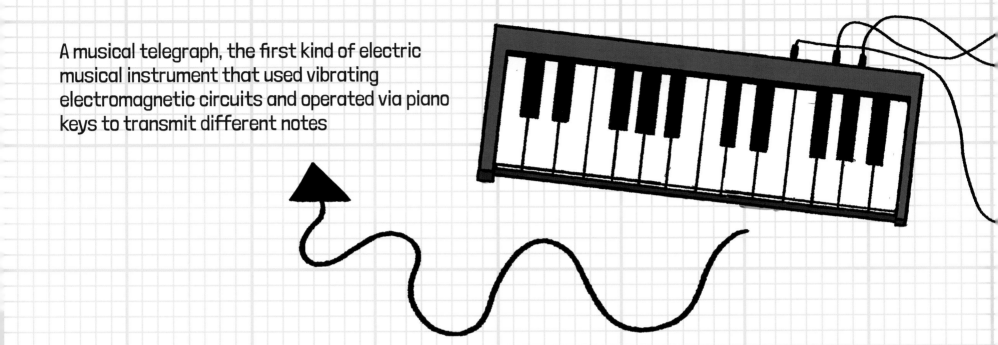

A telautograph, which could remotely transmit handwriting in a similar way to a telegraph transmitting Morse code—an early version of what we now know as a fax machine

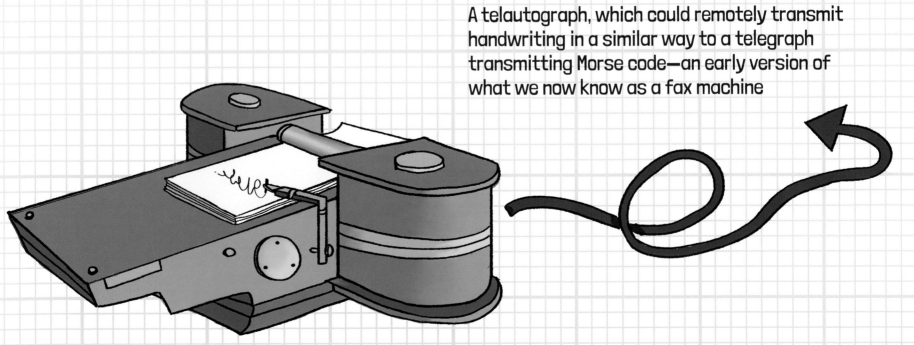

WORN-OUT WRITER

Elisha's passion for science could not be crushed by anything, whether it was a lack of formal education, struggling finances, or credit for inventing the telephone being awarded to someone else. He kept inventing until his death and, during his life, heavily promoted the sciences as something everyone should take an interest in.

During the 19th century, there was still widespread controversy between science and religion as times were rapidly changing during the Industrial Revolution. Elisha wrote a three-volume book called *Nature's Miracles*, in which he attempted to join science and religion and allow both to thrive together.

PROGRESS AND POSITIVITY

Unlike a lot of scientific books of the period, Elisha wrote *Nature's Miracles* using simple language and terms so it would be accessible to anyone who wanted to learn about science, regardless of formal education. During that time, lots of older people were frightened by quickly changing technology and ideas, and Elisha wanted everyone to gain a better understanding of science and how it helps us improve and to take away some of the stigma.

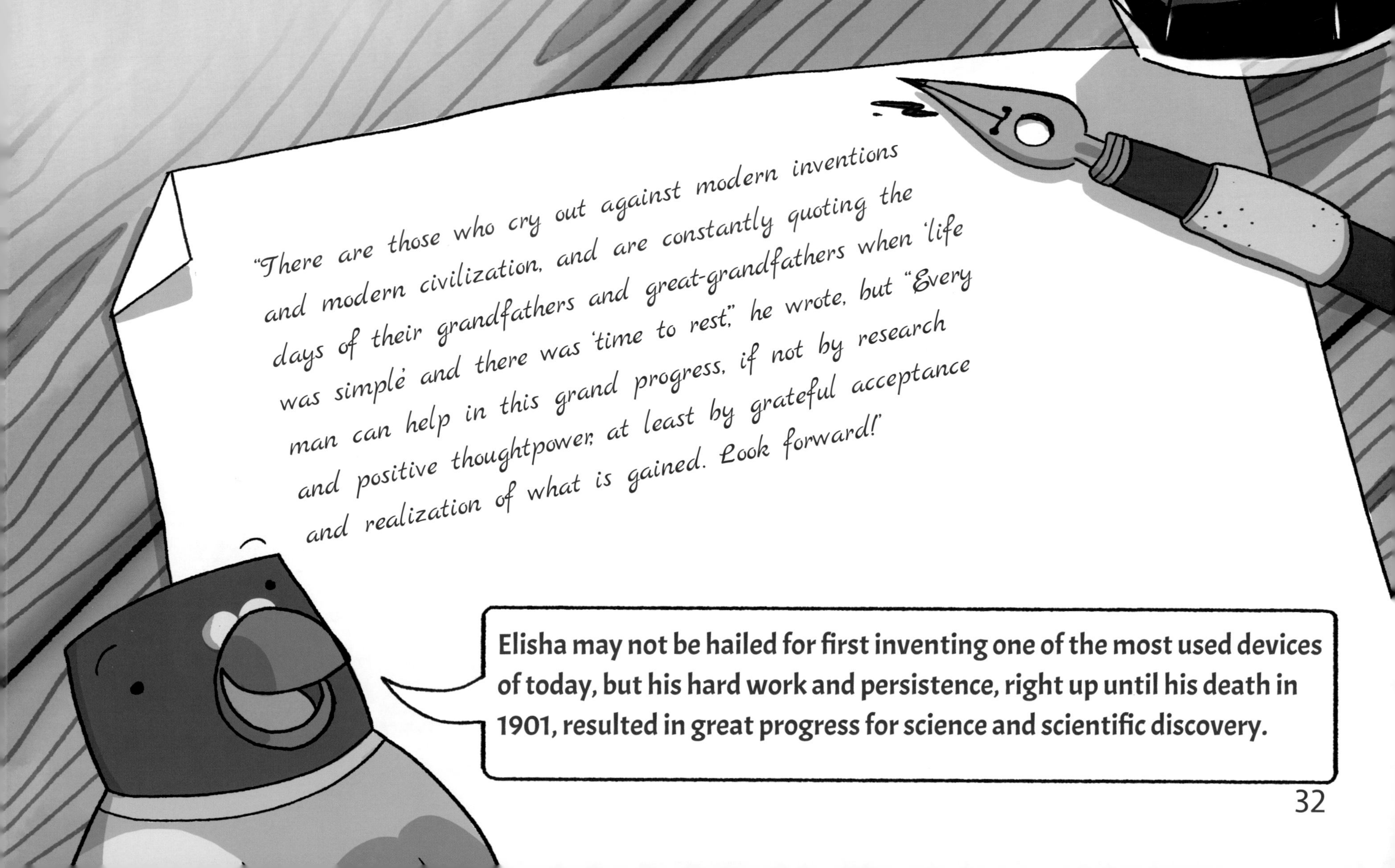
"There are those who cry out against modern inventions and modern civilization, and are constantly quoting the days of their grandfathers and great-grandfathers when 'life was simple' and there was 'time to rest,' he wrote, but "Every man can help in this grand progress, if not by research and positive thoughtpower, at least by grateful acceptance and realization of what is gained. Look forward!'
Elisha may not be hailed for first inventing one of the most used devices of today, but his hard work and persistence, right up until his death in 1901, resulted in great progress for science and scientific discovery.

ALEXANDER GRAHAM BELL

• Born in 1847 in Scotland.

• Went to school at the Royal High School at Edinburgh, was homeschooled, and studied at University College London, but did not finish his formal education.

• Worked with mute and deaf individuals for many years, teaching sign language, lip reading, and speech therapy.

• His first invention was made at age 12—a de-husking machine for a flour mill.

• Was funded by two wealthy patrons, Gardiner Hubbard, a lawyer who became his father-in-law, and Thomas Sanders, a rich leather merchant who was the father of one of his deaf students.

• Invented the world's first telephone.

• Had 18 inventions patented during his lifetime.

• His first words spoken through the telephone were to his assistant, Thomas Watson, and were: "Mr. Watson, come here. I want to see you."

ELISHA GRAY

- Born in 1835 in the USA.

- Left school at 12 and went back to school at 22, but never completed a formal education.

- Worked as a dairy farmer, blacksmith, carpenter, and janitor.

- His first invention was made at age 30—the self-adjusting telegraph relay.

- Was funded by a dentist named Dr. Samuel S. White.

- Invented the world's first musical telegraph.

- Had 70 inventions patented during his lifetime.

- Wrote a three-volume book about nature and science.

Oh no, it looks like the telegraph wires have gotten very tangled. Can you figure out which receiver is going to play the music?

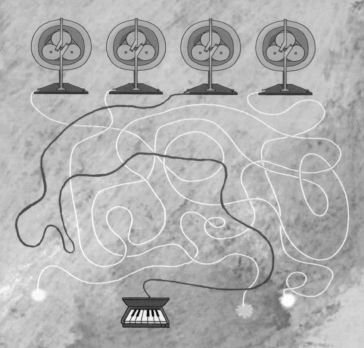

The examiners have a lot of patent applications to work through. Can you help them out by counting how many there are on this page?

14 patent applications

The race is on! How quickly can you find the route to the patent office?

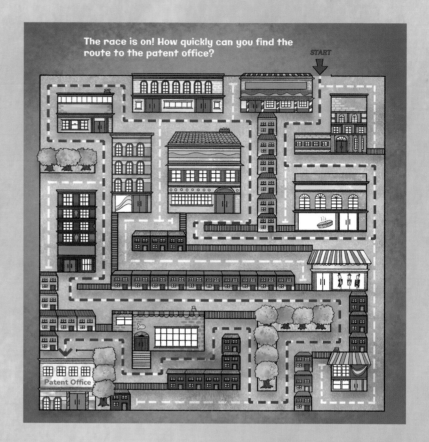

How many did you solve?

35